IMAGES OF WAR

GREAT PUSH

BATTLE OF
THE SOMME 1916

RARE PHOTOGRAPHS FROM WARTIME ARCHIVES

WILLIAM LANGLEY

First published in Great Britain in 2012 by
PEN & SWORD MILITARY
an imprint of
Pen & Sword Books Ltd,
47 Church Street, Barnsley,
South Yorkshire.
S70 2AS

ISBN 9781781590416

A CIP catalogue record for this book is available
from the British Library

Designed by Factionpress
Printed and bound by CPI Group (UK) Ltd, Croydon, CR0 4YY

Pen & Sword Books Ltd incorporates the imprints of
Pen & Sword Aviation, Pen & Sword Maritime,
Pen & Sword Military, Pen & Sword Select, Pen & Sword Military Classics,
Leo Cooper, Wharncliffe Local History

For a complete list of Pen & Sword titles please contact:
PEN & SWORD BOOKS LIMITED
47 Church Street, Barnsley, South Yorkshire, S70 2AS, England.
E-mail: enquiries@pen-and-sword.co.uk
Website: www.pen-and-sword.co.uk

Contents

Introduction **4**

Chapter One
Preparation and Great Expectations **7**

Chapter Two
Over The Top **55**

Chapter Three
Some Success – Mostly Failure **77**

Chapter Four
Some Small Pushes **101**

Chapter Five
Somme Winter **201**

Somme Chronology **233**

A British 18-pounder gun in action at Authuille Wood, September 1916. 1 GP/W078

Introduction

IT WAS TOO GOOD an opportunity to miss for many officers in the British Army when, in 1914 and 1915, they sailed across the Channel with the BEF – they took their cameras with them to record the historic events unfolding in Europe. Soon photographs of British soldiers in the trenches began to appear in newspapers and magazines throughout this country. The War Office decided it had to be stopped – far too much information presented on a plate to the enemy. Official cameramen – only – would take the images the nation thirsted for, thus control would be firmly with the authority conducting the war. Otherwise, illicit cameras were banned. This action coincided with the Allies' planned offensive against the German areas of occupation of France. In 1916 Sir Douglas Haig, commanding the BEF, began his great offensive to drive the invaders off the ground they had been occupying for over a year and a half. The 'Great Push' as the offensive was advertized to the nation, began 1 July 1916. A glossy picture magazine was produced to inform the British public of the progress of the offensive. Over a four month period, until the

Battle of the Somme faded away in November 1916, the magazine appeared with the following announcement on its title page:

Sir Douglas Haig's Great Push; The Battle of the Somme; A popular, pictorial and authoritative work on one of the Greatest Battles in History, illustrated by about 700 wonderful Official Photographs and Cinematograph Films; By Arrangement With the War Office; beautifully printed on the Best English Art Paper.

As is well known, the Great Push turned out to be little more than a vicious nudge but, for the sake of national morale, the British public had to be encouraged to believe that all was going well, especially in view of the horrific casualties wrecking the lives of families throughout the land.

The *Great Push*, in the form of *Images of War*, helps capture the British propaganda thrust of the times and presents once more the illustrations of those bewildering days along with an ID number for easy reference.

Taylor collection

Images from the Taylor Library have been included to help the pictorial history and they, along with images from the magazine, will reintroduce to public awareness the crafted camera work of those days of the Great War. This *Images of War* publication will serve as a catalogue for illustrations now available in the Taylor archive. An identifying number is included with the captions.

GERMAN SECOND

BRITISH FOURTH ARMY

Front Line
June 1916

Front Line
June 1916

Right is a part of the introduction to the magazine *Sir Douglas Haig's Great Push* which clearly demonstrates the optimistic spirit felt by the Allied command and transmitted to the people in Britain and the Empire who would be making the tremendous human sacrifice in this realm of Christendom with the blessing of the churches.

'THE EARLY PART of the winter of 1915-16 in the West was a period of almost complete stagnation. With the approach of spring there was a great increase of activity. At the end of February the Germans commenced their great attack on Verdun, where every yard of ground they gained was dyed red with German blood. On the British front there was some fierce fighting in the Ypres salient, in which the Canadians again greatly distinguished themselves, and also about Neuve Chapelle, which resulted in substantial gain of ground, and was regarded as a happy augury for the coming [British] offensive. On the first day of June the great naval battle off the coast of Jutland afforded one more proof of the immeasurable superiority of the British seaman over the German.

'A few days later, 6 June, to the inexpressible grief of the whole Empire, the cruiser *Hampshire*, which was on her way to Russia with Lord Kitchener on board, went down off the Orkneys. But our grief at the tragic end of the great soldier was tempered by the reflection that his work had been practically accomplished, and that nothing remained for us but to set in motion the mighty machine which his genius had created and perfected.'

HMS *Hampshire* sank off the Orkneys on 6 June 1916 with the loss of Lord Kitchener and 643 sailors.
The face of Kitchener, as a national hero and personality, was used to appeal for volunteers.

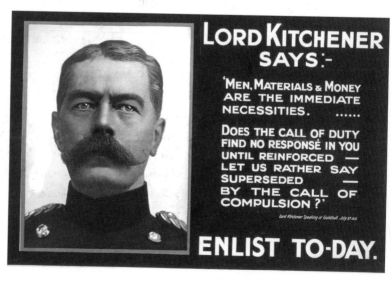

Chapter One

Preparation and Great Expectations

The official journalists and authors who produced the text for the magazine *Great Push* naturally assumed that the British generals had learned important lessons over the previous two years – officially – they were committed to make that assumption. Certainly experience should have taught the generals how to mount an offensive with reasonable expectations of success and without incurring massive loss of life. The Great Push on the Somme was being planned by the General Staff in the light of such bitterly gained experience.

It may be of interest to historians to note the expectations of the writers:

'TOWARDS THE END OF JUNE, 1916, it became apparent that the moment was at hand when the 'Big Push' on the Western Front, so long expected and so ardently desired, might at length be attempted with every prospect of success. For months the Allied Staffs had been making ready for this stage. Never has the world witnessed preparation on so colossal a scale – a preparation which had converted Great Britain into a vast arsenal and a first-class military power – and it is hardly conceivable that the world will ever witness the like again. But it was known that the enemy, too, had not wasted these months, and that we should do well to presume that every device or plan that military genius can conceive or apply for the strengthening and elaboration of their system of defences must have been carried out with the greatest thoroughness and scientific precision; that every eventuality that could be foreseen had been provided against.

'In the great Champagne and Artois offensives of last year our advance was in nearly every case successful as regards the first line of the enemy's trenches; but it was thereafter frequently held up by local centres of resistance which had survived our preliminary bombardment, and rarely effected any serious breach in the second lines; while the casualties sustained were very heavy. Happily, we had not failed to profit by the experience so dearly purchased, and, recognizing that artillery had become the decisive arm so long as the present fixed lines exist, and that it was only when our artillery and its provisions were at length superior that we could hope for success, we resolved to wait until the huge national effort thrown into the output of munitions under the auspices of Mr Lloyd George had progressed sufficiently to become a chief factor in Armageddon. *Never again, if it could by any possibility be prevented, must our heroic infantry find themselves, when they approached within sight of their goal, come up against unbroken lines of wire, and unsuspected shelters from which cunningly concealed machine guns spat unceasing streams of lead. Never again must they be forced to relinquish the ground which their valour had won because the trenches into which they had fought their way were rendered untenable by the fire of [enemy] batteries which an adequate artillery preparation should have enabled us to destroy.'*

Above in italics is ours. The British nation was being prepared to expect something different by way of achieving victory over the Germans. Fresh troops forming new divisions had been raised and the country's menfolk could expect to be employed in warfare with a high degree of military skill acquired through costly experience. 'Never again' would British soldiers face uncut wire and machine guns. And those at home who encouraged and supported their enlisting were being encouraged to entertain great expectations.

In the weeks prior to the 'Great Advance' divisions of infantry and cavalry moved into position in the countryside above the Somme River. 160GP

Army Service Corps behind the British lines opposite the German held village of Fricourt-Mametz. 161GP

A platoon of the Buffs (East Kents) answering roll call in the village of Bray prior to leaving for the trenches. 162GP

Men of the Bedfordshire Regiment moving up on the evening of the attack. 163GP

Royal Artillery horses being watered. 'Casualties among horses have been very heavy.' 167GP

Motorcycle combination pulls into a used shell case dump. 169GP

Royal Field Artillery with their mascot, a captured fox. 168GP

French peasants working the fields as preparations for the attack go on all around.

General Sir Henry Rawlinson, commanding the British Fourth Army, had been given his objectives by General Sir Douglas Haig: 'relieving the pressure on the French at Verdun and inflicting loss on the enemy'. Further, preparations were to be made for an advance of seven miles to Bapaume should German resistance crumble. 'If the first attack goes well every effort must be made to develop the success to the utmost by firstly opening a way for our cavalry and then as quickly as possible pushing the cavalry through to seize Bapaume.'

Rawlinson prepared to carry out his orders by first bombarding the enemy relentlessly for a week with a million and a half shells.

Unloading boxes of 25 pdr shells and passing them by human chain to gun limbers. These frames are from the film version of the *Great Push*. 170GP 171GP 172GP

The 18-pounder was first produced in 1904. In August 1914, the British Army had 1,226 of them. By the end of the war, the army had upwards of nine and a half thousand in service. Above: Carnoy Valley 30 July. Below: 18-pounders at Authuille, September 1916. 124GP, 84BP

Neat stacks of 18-pounder shells. 87BP, 87BPa

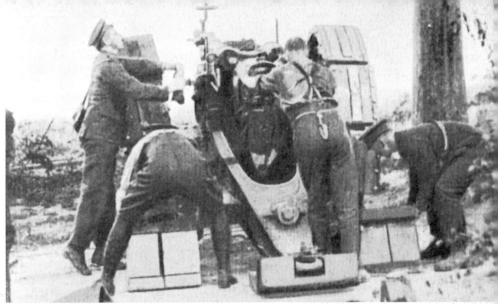

Film sequence showing
British 4.7 inch gun in
action firing on the
German-held village of
Mametz June 1916.
Top: being sighted.
Centre: about to be fired.
Bottom: recoil.
144GP

Empty shell cases – a
graphic image indicating
the amount of explosives
being hurled at the
German positions prior to
the Great Push 88BP

A sequence showing
stages in the firing of a
British 4.7 inch gun.
174GP, 175GP

Taking up a 60-pounder artillery piece with a twelve-horse team. 18BP
Man-handling the 60-pounder into position. 17BP

Three views from inside a Canadian 60-pounder position and shells bursting on the German trenches.
185GP
186GP

Canadian 60-pounder in a well protected position. 125BP

Moment of firing. 125BP

Preparing to load a 15-inch howitzer using a chain hoist system to lift the shells. It could throw a 1,400 lb heavy shell six miles and some considered it hardly worth all the labour and time it took to move and emplace these very heavy guns. 122BP 139BP

One round a
minute could be
achieved by a good
gun crew. 139BP
123BP

Above, the 9.2-inch howitzer which could lob a shell a distance of five and a half miles. 'Little brother' to the 15-inch howitzer pictured left. 130BP 138BP

Ammunition for the mighty 15-inch howitzers.   GP001   216GP   215GP

The 9.2-inch howitzer filmed
during firing. 200GP 201GP

Shells for the mighty
15-inch howitzer. 206GP

Left: Ramming home a shell into the breech of the 12-inch Mk1 howitzer, or 'Grandmother', manned by the Royal Marine Artillery. 203GP

Below: Ready to fire. 217GP

Left: The 12-inch howitzer after firing. 205GP

Moving an 8-inch howitzer to a new position, summer 1916.
129BP

The BL 8-inch howitzer Mark I, a British improvization developed to provide heavy artillery. It used shortened and bored-out barrels from various redundant naval 6-inch guns. It remained in use on the Western Front throughout the war. 121BP

Camouflaged howitzer position. 120BP

A 9.2-inch railway gun. 222BP

Bombs for the 2-inch Medium Trench Mortar, also known as the 2-inch howitzer, and nicknamed the 'Toffee Apple' or 'Plum Pudding' mortar.
196GP 198GP 199GP

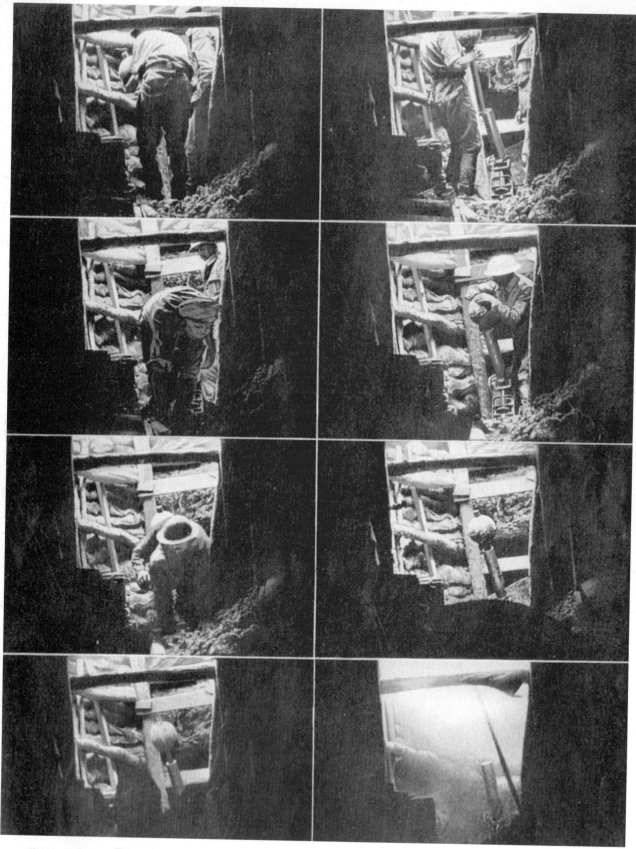

Firing plum puddings into the German trenches. 197GP

Loading sequence: 1, the catch of the 9.45-inch trench mortar is released enabling it to be revolved 2, 3, 4, 5. The barrel is lowered and the weapon is loaded 6; it is then raised 7 and swung back to its former position 8, 9, 10. The crew retire 11 and the weapon is fired 12.   213GP 214GP

A British shell exploding among the German barbed wire. It was thought that the five-day bombardment of the German positions would destroy the wire. In some places it did, but it could be easily replaced at night by the Germans. 202GP 128BP

Men of the Royal Flying Corps bringing up a 'nurse balloon'. It was used to transport the large quantity of gas required to inflate an observation balloon. 55BP

An observation balloon being prepared. 54BP

Becoming airborn – a Caquot Kite Balloon about to ascend. 76BP

Opposite: 'Lift-off' the flight is under way. 92BP

Intrepid observer checks that his telephone line is linked up and working before ascending. 47BP

Signal exchange relaying information from observation posts and balloons to various headquarters and artillery positions. 93BP

Playing with the French – a tug of war between British and French artillery personnel. These were likely men of the 30th Division, 89 Brigade, near Maricourt facing the German positions in front of Montauban. This was the extreme right of the British Army on the Somme where it met the French Army. 59BP

Men of a Highland regiment threshing their own straw for fodder and bedding. 85BP

War horses – officers' mounts await their masters at a British artillery position on the Somme. 180BP

Cavalry fully expected to be used to exploit the breakthrough that would occur. 60BP

Indian cavalry waiting to advance during the second week of the Great Push. 98BP 99BP

Indian cavalry practise their cavalry charge behind the lines on the Somme front. 158GP

Cavalry on the move behind the lines on the Somme front. 319GP

Bringing up supplies for the Great Push. 115BP

General Sir Beauvoir de Lisle addresses a battalion of the 29th Division on the eve of the battle. 145BP

A battalion at Church Parade receive assurance from the padre that the Almighty is on their side. This will lead to bitter disillusion for many when the Germans, wearing the slogan *Gott Mit Uns*, (God With Us), inflict heavy casualties and British attacks meet with little success. 192GP

A battalion of the East Yorkshire Regiment marching to take their place at the front. 193GP 195GP

Middle four pictures are of the Royal Welsh Fusiliers moving through a French village on the eve of the attack. 134GP

1/14th (County of London) Battalion London Scottish marching to take position for the diversionary attack on Gommecourt by the 56th (Territorial) Division. 187BP 188BP

Men of the 1st Battalion, Wiltshire Regiment, greet the camera as they march along the Acheux road to the trenches. 190GP

Men of the Worcestershire Regiment on the Acheux road leading to the trenches. 1GP/W001

A battalion of the Hampshire Regiment with (below) stretcher bearers bringing up the rear. Note the 'clown' taking a bow for the camera. 178BP 179BP

Lewis Gun section of the 10th Battalion, East Yorkshire Regiment, near Doullens July 1916. 184BP

A battalion of the Royal Warwickshire Regiment resting during a route march to the trenches. 210GP

Men of the Worcestershire Regiment take a break during the march to the front. 209GP

Troops earmarked as reserves moving up to their positions. 208GP

Australian troops gathered for the Somme offensive. Their involvement took place between 23 July and 3 September and involved attacks at Pozières and Mouquet Farm. As the Great Push fizzled out in November 1916 they were involved in the futile attacks around Flers. 287GP

Australian troops drawing water for their artillery unit. 316GP

General William Riddell Birdwood, commanding I Anzac Corps, meets some of the Anzac soldiers under his command. 300GP

Monkey mascot of these Anzac troops photographed on horseback. 253GP

Australian pioneers filling sandbags. 104BP

Australians resting on their way to the trenches. 221GP

New Zealand troops queue for supplies. 61BP

Anzac cooks preparing a meal. 50BP

Australians with mascot coming out of the line for a rest.   75BP

Wiring party going to the front line trenches after collecting stores. 191GP

Vickers machine-gun
post just behind a
front line trench.
223GP 224GP

See opposite.
226GP

Dawn on 1 July and artillery shells reached a cresendo. All the British infantry would have to do was to walk over and take the battered German trenches. 218GP 219GP

Men of a Royal Engineers Tunnelling Company deep underground beneath the chalking soil of the Somme laying an explosive charge. The officer with the instrument called the geophone is listening for any sounds that would warn of Germans digging a counter-mine called a *camouflet*. 232GP

Chapter Two

Over The Top

The magazine *Great Push* reported events as they unfolded as the largest assault in the history of warfare, to date, began on Saturday morning 1 July 1916. The Franco-British attack had been fully expected to succeed and the overwhelming of the German defences was supposed to be occuring along a twenty-five mile front. It was not happening, apart from in the south where the British-held line butted up to the French. British 30th Division, which comprised mainly Manchester and Liverpool Pals battalions, swept through – as envisaged by the planning generals – and captured the German-held village of Montauban. Also there was success in capturing the village of Mametz by the 7th Division and then Fricourt the following day. Elsewhere along the front it was a disaster. The truth of the situation was distorted as the magazine covered the attack. What the writer did not have by way of accurate military information, he made up with creative writing.

'WITH A TERRIFIC ROAR a deep mine, packed with many tons of the highest explosives known to science, was exploded near La Boisselle, blowing a great gap in the enemy's defences, and a part of the Royal Engineers rushed off to wire the crater for occupation by our advance troops. Just before 7.30am our gunners lengthened their range and began to interpose a terrific barrage of fire between the enemy's first and second lines. No reinforcements could possibly make their way through that hail of shell. At the same time, clouds of smoke were liberated to form a screen for our infantry, who punctually at the half-hour swarmed out of their trenches and, with a mighty cheer, advanced to the attack. The 'Great Push' had begun!

'In modern warfare, with large assemblages of troops and regular artillery preparations, surprise is exceedingly difficult, and the enemy were in no degree taken unawares. The best evidence goes to show that they had been expecting our attack to be delivered that morning, though they appear to have ante-dated it by a couple of hours. Since daybreak, indeed, certain sectors of our front had been heavily and continuously shelled, and the discharge of the smoke clouds was the signal for No Man's Land to be swept by a hurricane of lead from countless machine guns. But, thanks to the smoke, it was blind shooting, and, though not a few of our men fell before even they had crossed our parapet, they were the victims of chance bullets.

'On through the tempest of death swept our brave fellows; men fell at every step, but their comrades kept steadily on; the more casualties they saw in front of them, the louder they cheered, the faster they pressed forward; and at 11:55am Sir Douglas Haig was able to report that "British troops have broken into German forward system of defences along a front of sixteen miles." For along great stretches of the enemy's lines our bombardment had wrought enormous damage, sweeping away the barbed wire, flattening the parapets, and blowing in the dugouts, which in many places were found choked with dead bodies. Frequently, out of those dug-outs which had survived the storm of high explosives crept dazed and deafened men, who surrendered without a semblance of resistance; indeed, at one part of the line the Germans did not even wait for our men to enter their trenches, but emerging from their shelters as soon as the British guns lifted, met the advancing troops in the open, holding up their hands in token of surrender.'

The truth was, that north-west of the Albert-Bapaume road the British made little progress against the German defences, apart for a small gain at the Leipzig Redoubt to the south of Thiepval. They had failed and been turned back in front of the German fortified villages of Gommecourt, Serre, Beaumont Hamel, Thiepval and La Boisselle. Casualties were a staggering 57,000, the highest casualty figure ever suffered by the British Army.

The futile struggle to push German forces holding high ground positions off French territory placed about the River Somme would go on until November.

Awaiting the mine to explode under Hawthorne Ridge to signal the attack.   225GP 1GP/002

1 GP/W002

Well known image of British soldiers on the Somme. It has been claimed that the seated figure in the foreground is a Private Bailey, 12th Battalion, (Sheffield City) York and Lancaster Regiment.

1 GP/W037

Fix bayonets! Lancashire Fusiliers ready for the walk across No Man's Land.
I GP/W004 I GP/W003

Before dawn on 1 July 1st Battalion Lancashire Fusiliers entered this sunken lane in No Man's Land to use it as a jumping off position for the attack on Beaumont Hamel. As they left this cover at 7.30am they came under converging machine-gun fire from Beaumont Hamel and Hawthorn Ridge. Eighteen officers and 465 men were lost during the day's fighting. 229GPa

Ten minutes before zero the mine was blown giving the Germans, who had rushed to occupy the crater caused by the explosion, sufficient time to prepare to meet the attacking British infantry. At 7.30am men of the 29th Division left their trenches and walked into a hail of death.
1GP/W003

In front of and attacking the German fortified village of La Boisselle was 34th Division. The Northumberland Fusiliers – Tyneside Irish – are seen here about to enter No Man's Land with their rifles slung on their shoulders. IGP/W005

As the leading wave moves off the second wave can be seen about to stand up and follow. IGP/W006

The mines went off and a few minutes later 103 Brigade began coming over the hill in beautifully regular lines, dressing and intervals maintained as well as on a ceremonial parade. Everyone felt proud of that lot of Tynesiders. Battalion history of the Pioneers, 18th Northumberland Fusiliers.

Y Sap Crater, one of two mines blown in this sector on 1 July under German positions. The attack was not successful, despite the mines and losses sustained, particularly by the Tyneside Scottish, and other battalions of the 34th Division were heavy. The ground is littered with dead and wounded men from Tyneside. LB1

Men of the Wiltshire Regiment passing through their own wire as they are launched against the fortified village of Thiepval. The German fortified village would finally fall in September. 1GP/W007

British troops, believed to be the 2nd Battalion, Gordon Highlanders (7th Division) crossing No Man's Land near Mametz on 1 July 1916. 114BP

After the morning attacks two companies of 2nd Royal Warwicks and two of 8th Devons attacked at 3.30pm; it was enough for the German garrison of Mametz: 200 of them surrendered before the new attack had even reached the old German front line. Just after 4pm, the village of Mametz had fallen and within a further hour the situation was quiet.   109BP

Village of Mametz after its capture 1 July 1916. 110BP

Image of British Tommies being swallowed up by smoke as they attack on 1 July. 229GPb

In among the ruins of Mametz. 264GP

Wounded German prisoner being helped through the British front line trench. 234GPa

German prisoners being searched behind the British trenches. Note the screens to hide activities from enemy observers. 151GP

Wrecked house in Mametz. This one had been sandbagged and used as a German strongpoint. 110BPa

The main street through Mametz after a clean-up following its capture. 149GP

Dead Germans caught in the shelling of their trenches. 159GP

The movie camera records wounded being brought in from No Man's Land. 1 GP/W008

The original caption for this iconic image for the 1 July disaster informs us that this soldier brought in from No Man's Land twenty wounded men. 152GP

231GPa

231GPb

231GPc

231GPd

1GP/W009a

1GP/W009b

1GP/W0010

On 1 July 1916 all along the Somme front the British trenches became clogged with wounded Tommies. A disaster was unfolding before the camera lens as stretcher bearers struggled to carry wounded comrades through the congested communication trenches to the Advanced Dressing Stations.

IGP/W0011

248GPa

Minden Post, 7th Division area
where lightly wounded men of 91
Brigade receive treatment.
The soldier being treated has been
wounded in the left arm, which
shows bullet entry and exit
wounds. He also appears to have
been injured on his right shoulder.

248GPb

248GPc

248GP

246GP

247GPa

Walking wounded leaving Minden Post. In the background are soldiers of the 24th Battalion, Manchester Regiment 'Oldham Comrades' (Pioneers), awaiting orders to advance and develop captured German trenches at Fricourt.

247GPb

220GP

247GPc

A German medical orderly among this group of prisoners at the Advance Dressing Station.

247GPd

245GP

245GPab

234GP

Chapter Three

Some Success – Mostly Failure

With things not going the way that had been expected in the way of objectives taken, and with a staggering casualty list which made 1 July 1916 the blackest day ever in the history of the British Army, concentration by the reporters on the small successes was understandable. Coverage by the *Great Push* magazine in areas of total failure was refreshingly frank, with reasons for the lack of success given along with optimistic predictions for future offensive operations. The true story was becoming all too clear in towns and cities throughout Britain as telegrams arrived at the homes of thousands who had their menfolk embroiled in Haig's Great Push on the Somme. Local weekly newspapers carried lists of dead and missing; many pages reproduced portraits of the fallen. Letters from officers and chaplains from the units in which men had served began flooding into the country. Invariably, the deaths were instantaneous; the deceased were always well respected, fine soldiers and brave; they would be missed by their comrades; their lives sacrificed in a worthy cause; also they had been buried well behind the lines with a cross marking the grave. It would have been heartless to say anything else. Those who were suffering loss of their loved ones could find explanations of the fighting and glory in such magazines as the *Great Push*.

'ABOUT THE GOMMECOURT SALIENT the German defences were as perfect as defences could well be, their dugouts being so deep and so solidly built that they were practically indestructible. The enemy had concentrated a great mass of artillery and an enormous number of machine guns here in the belief that the British main attack was to extend from Lille to Roye. The big guns barraged our front with a most infernal fire; while the machine guns were in position within a few seconds of our bombardment lifting, and so numerous were these deadly weapons that their clamour as they spat their streams of lead amongst our advancing troops is said to have actually drowned the noise of the artillery. In the places where the rain of bombs from our trench mortars was smothering their trenches the enemy, with great courage, came out into No Man's Land and worked their guns in the open.

'Through this inferno of bullets and explosives our troops advanced as steadily as on parade, not a man faltering, save those who fell, and with bomb and bayonet forced their way into and across the German first-line trenches, on wards to their second line, and even in places to their third. But, under the murderous fire to which they were exposed their losses were so great that no lasting success was possible: they could not hold the ground they had won, and though a party of some one hundred men belonging to a Lancashire battalion actually succeeded in fighting their way into a village bristling with machine guns beyond the enemy's third line, at a point south-east of Hébuterne, they appear to have been entirely wiped out, since not one of them was seen again.*

'All this time, from every part of the long battle-front, a continual stream of wounded men was flowing back to the casualty clearing stations behind the British lines. The serious cases were brought back on stretchers; the others walked back unaided or with the assistance of comrades, often wounded themselves, or rode on lorries, which had taken up ammunition and were now bringing back casualties, sometimes fifty or more on one lorry.

> "They are wonderful men, so wonderful in their gaiety and courage that one's heart melted at the sight of them. They were all grinning as though they had come from a jolly in which they had been bumped a little. There was a look of pride in their eyes as they came driving down like wounded knights from a tourney. They had gone through the job with honour and had come out with their lives, and the world was good and beautiful again in this warm sun... The men who were going up to the battle grinned back at those who were coming back. The laughing men on the lorries – some of them stripped to the waist and bandaged roughly – seemed to rob the war of some its horrors; and the spirit of our British soldiers shines very bright along the roads of France, so that the very sun seems to get some of its gold from these men's hearts."
> – Philip Gibbs, *Daily Chronicle*.

'The principal achievement of the second day of the great battle was the capture of Fricourt.

'The village, like Mametz and Montauban, was a heap of ruins while the trenches in many places were simply pounded to bits. Behind the remnant of one parapet lay a German grenadier, still clasping in his clenched right hand the grenade he was about to throw when death overtook him. Further away was a group of three infantrymen, who had been struck down together by a shell and half buried beneath a fallen wall. In every corner, in every shell hole or wrecked dugout, were dead and yet more dead.'

---

*This account of British troops entering 'a village' was reported by an observer in an aeroplane of the Royal Flying Corps and must be referring to men of the 11th Battalion, East Lancashire Regiment (Accrington Pals) who were attacking the German fortified village of Serre along with the 12th Battalion, York & Lancaster Regiment (Sheffield City Battalion); 14th Battalion, York & Lancaster Regiment (2nd Barnsley Pals) and 13th Battalion, York & Lancaster Regiment (1st Barnsley Pals). Brigadier General Hubert C. Rees, commander of 94 Brigade, could not bring himself to believe the report. He stopped further reinforcements following up the attack on Serre, thus accepting failure and saving lives of men under his command.

A Company Sergeant Major, Lancashire Fusiliers, takes a roll call of the survivors.
I GP/W013

Captured trenches showing the entrances to the deep underground living quarters. This was the German line at La Boisselle where men of the 34th and 8th Divisions fought to capture, 1 July.
9BP

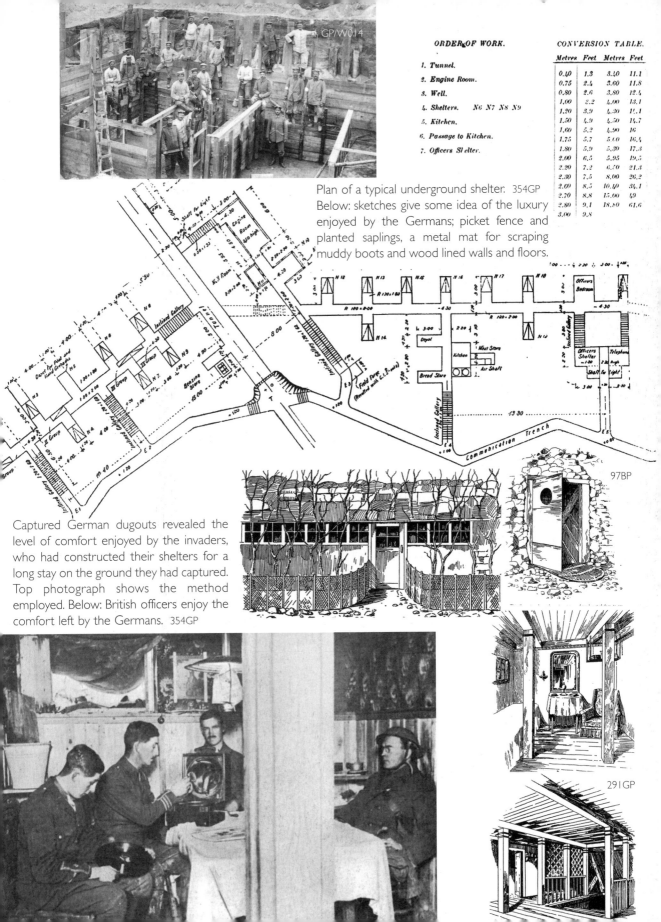

ORDER OF WORK.

1. *Tunnel.*
2. *Engine Room.*
3. *Well.*
4. *Shelters.* N6 N7 N8 N9
5. *Kitchen.*
6. *Passage to Kitchen.*
7. *Officers Shelter.*

CONVERSION TABLE.

Metres	Feet	Metres	Feet
0.40	1.3	3.40	11.1
0.75	2.4	3.60	11.8
0.80	2.6	3.80	12.4
1.00	3.2	4.00	13.1
1.20	3.9	4.30	14.1
1.50	4.9	4.50	14.7
1.60	5.2	4.90	16
1.75	5.7	5.00	16.4
1.80	5.9	5.30	17.3
2.00	6.5	5.95	19.5
2.20	7.2	6.70	21.3
2.30	7.5	8.00	26.2
2.60	8.5	10.40	34.1
2.70	8.8	15.00	49
2.80	9.1	18.80	61.6
3.00	9.8		

Plan of a typical underground shelter. 354GP
Below: sketches give some idea of the luxury enjoyed by the Germans; picket fence and planted saplings, a metal mat for scraping muddy boots and wood lined walls and floors.

Captured German dugouts revealed the level of comfort enjoyed by the invaders, who had constructed their shelters for a long stay on the ground they had captured. Top photograph shows the method employed. Below: British officers enjoy the comfort left by the Germans. 354GP

97BP

291GP

German machine gun position destroyed by a British shell near Guillemont. Note the corporal who seems to have acquired a German officer's pistol and leather holster. 31BP

Right: shells failed to cave in the deep shelters. British soldiers have taken occupation. 289GP

Built to last, these steps lead to underground positions at at the northern corner of Bernafay Wood. It was captured 3 July by men of the 9th Division.
327GP

Below: this was once the French village of Ginchy, fortified by the Germans, now occupied by the British.
326GP

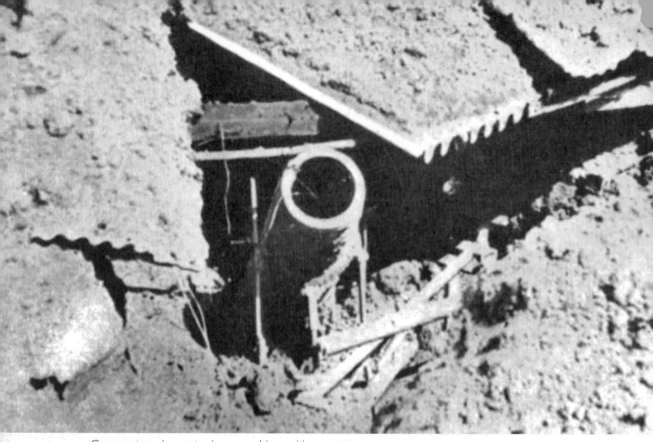

German trench mortar in a caved-in position. 244GP

Captured prisoners in cages. 349GP

Some of the first prisoners taken on 1 July 1916. 137BP

This prisoner-of-war cage was at St Pierre Divion. 388GP

German prisoners passing the time with a game of chess. 372GP

German prisoners
seemingly pleased that
for them the war is
over. 349GP

Prisoners leaving for
England. 277GP

Men of the Sherwood Foresters wearing pickelhaube helmets, Luger pistols and bayonets captured from the Germans. 285GP

Captured German trench mortars. 265GP 266GP

Artillery men examine a captured German 77mm Field Gun M96nA. This was the principal field gun built by Krupp and was used throughout the war.
116BP

Captured by men of the 7th Division.
269GP

Left: A Belgian Army 57mm Nordenfeldt captured and used by the Germans. It was captured by the British 7th Division and is seen here being taken away by the Royal Artillery. 268GP

Below (left to right): Danish Madsen light machine gun; Russian Maxim heavy machine gun; German Maxim 08; trench mortar. 119BPa

Bottom: items captured in the early days of the advance: two periscopes with cases; one field telephone; one gas helmet.
119BP

German prisoners set to work cleaning up their weapons. 86BP
Trench mortar bound for the Royal Engineers Depot at Chatham. 1BP

Captured field guns and heavy trench mortars. 150GP

View of the breech mechanism of this cleaned up German field gun. 3BP

2BP

1BP

4BP

4BP

Collecting together weapons after an attack: German 08 Maxims are being examined by these Tommies.
376GP

Salvaged British rifles being collected following an attack. 330GP

Rifles collected and stacked after a British attack. Many have bayonets fixed and were recently carried by those who became casualties. 330GP
A daunting task for the armourers. 395GP

Large packs of casualties – not carried by the attacking soldier – have to be sorted through. They usually contained the soldier's great coat and blanket, along with personal effects. | GP/W016

Wounded from the Somme battles could be treated on one of the hospital barges moored along the French canals. A precarious passage aboard for this wounded soldier via, in the circumstances, a rather narrow gangplank. 26BP

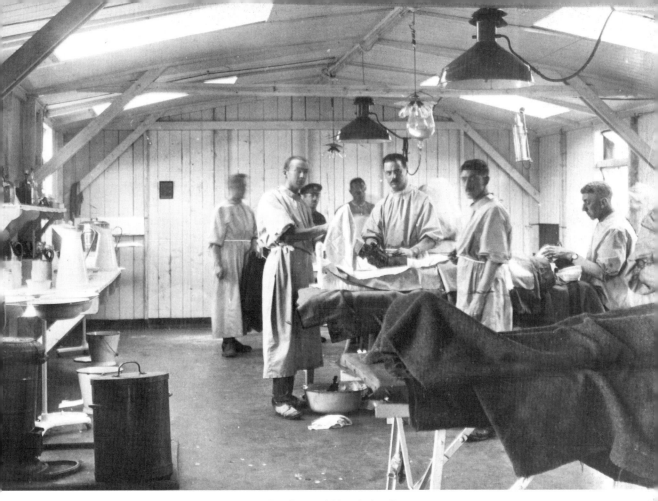

Serious operations being carried out at the General Hospital at Base. I GP/W017

Some of the many wounded soldiers recuperating back in England. BP Ia

Words are read over the graves of two Tommies killed in the fighting near Orvillers, July 1916.
1 GP/W019

Orderly burials took place near aid posts where men died of their wounds.
364GP

Scattered British graves at High Wood.
1 GP/W018

Chapter Four

Some Small Pushes

During the first two weeks of the Push the fighting had degenerated into a series of small-scale actions which, it was hoped, would develop into a breakthrough. From 3 to 13 July, Rawlinson's Fourth Army carried out upwards of fifty small offensive engagements resulting in 25,000 casualties, with no significant advance. This demonstrated a difference in strategy between Haig and his French counterparts and was a source of friction. The British generals purposed to maintain continual pressure on the Germans while, on the other hand, Joffre and Foch preferred to conserve their strength for a single, heavy blow. Success attained by the French in the Allied Somme offensive far outweighed that of the British; the French Sixth Army had advanced six miles (10km) taking 12,000 prisoners and assorted weapons and materials, all with minimal losses.

'WE HAD NOW REACHED THE DIFFICULT PERIOD which invariably follows a successful offensive movement, when ground gained has to be consolidated under the savaging of the enemy's artillery; no attempt at a further general advance was made on the 16th, while the Germans appeared to be awaiting the arrival of reinforcements before renewing their counter-attacks. The guns on both sides, however, were very active, notwithstanding that a thick mist lay over the countryside, causing what naval men call "low visibility," and rendering artillery observation difficult. The British batteries shelled High Wood, from which our troops had been withdrawn at daybreak, and pounded the enemy's lines to the north of Bazentin-le-Grand and Longueval, while the German guns retaliated upon the villages and woodlands we had captured and held during the past three days. All that day we continued to find large quantities of armament and other war material which had been abandoned by the enemy in the positions taken by the British.

'Sir Douglas Haig reported that the captured armament collected by our troops now included five 8-inch howitzers, three 6-inch howitzers, four 6-inch guns, five other heavy weapons, thirty-seven field-guns, thirty trench-howitzers, sixty-six machine guns, and many thousands of rounds of gun ammunition of all descriptions. He added that the above was exclusive of many guns not yet brought in, and of the pieces destroyed by our artillery bombardment and abandoned by the enemy. In the same communique he announced that the total of unwounded German prisoners captured since 1 July was 189 officers and 10,779 non-commissioned officers and men.'

Often seen image of British infantry in a captured trench. A sentry keeps on the watch for a possible German counter-attack while his comrades grab some sleep. Men of the 11th Battalion The Cheshire Regiment, near La Boisselle.   I GP/W020

Working party of a Highland regiment clearing and repairing a road to help consolidate the gains.
368GP 370GP

The importance of a steady supply of water to an army in the field can be seen here. Water containers bring fresh supplies by a light railway. 324GP
Pipes are being laid to bring water to the these gun positions. 288GP

Petrol cans filled with water is the method being used here to take the vital supply through the trenches to the fighting men. 2909GP

Underground pipeline bringing water to a narrow gauge rail line. 1 GP/W021

A War Department Light Railway 0-6-0 Hudson with some early C-type wagons at Fricourt.. 333GP

The *Scotch Express* was one of the earliest petrol tractors used over the light railway system and it was made from motor car parts. 336GP

Man-powered trolley hauling medical supplies to an Advance Dressing Station. 337GP

A 20 hp Simplex petrol tractor moving pre-fabricated track panels. 338GP

A standard gauge Manning Wardle petrol tractor, Bazentin-le-Grand. 69BP

Laying track to bring up supplies for the ongoing offensive. 331GP

Shrapnel-shredded French rolling stock. 81BP

Caught by artillery. 81BP

80BP

French civilian modes of transport riddled with shrapnel and bullets: a horse drawn cab and a taxi. 335GP 351GP

Having some fun for the camera – the cab has been given a destination. 30BP
One soldier has found a shaped backrest in this fallen bell from the church at Montauban. 339GP

Parcels and letters from home. A Royal Artillery man arrives with the post.
341GP

Settling into former German shelters.
126BP

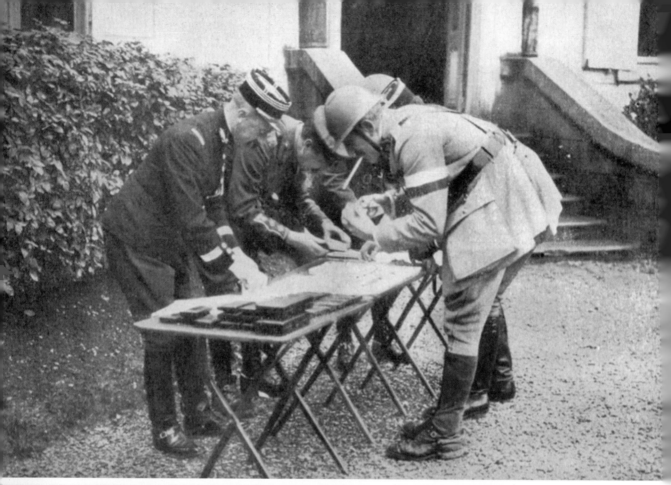

British and French officers prepare medals for an award ceremony to honour men who had acted with bravery during the Somme fighting.
378GP

An official French photographer prepares to take a portrait of a wounded soldier from a Highland regiment
357GP

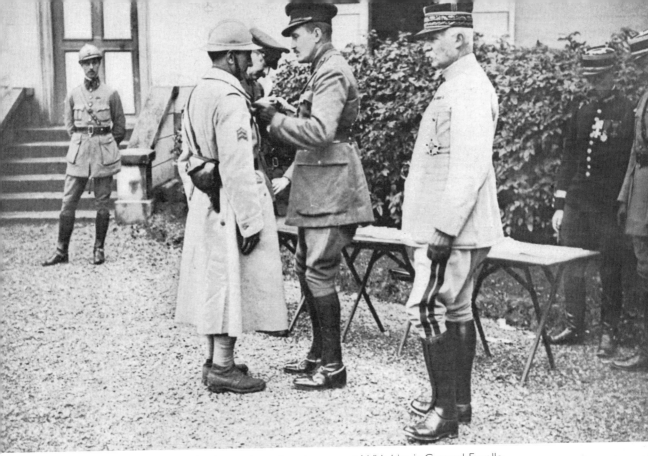

Prince Arthur of Connaught decorating a French sergeant. With him is General Fayolle, commanding the French Sixth Army. 90BP

French General Gourard inspects a British officers' training cadre at Base Camp 398GP

Prince Arthur of Connaught decorating a French general. 91BP

King George V visits France in August 1916. Left to right: General Joffre, President Poincaré, King George, General Foch and General Haig. 62BP

The King and Haig passing through Haig's bodyguard. The King is holding flowers presented by a little girl. 303GP

King Albert I of Belgium introduces some of his generals to King George V. 303GP

The King is greeted by a matron at an
Advanced Operative Centre. 305GP

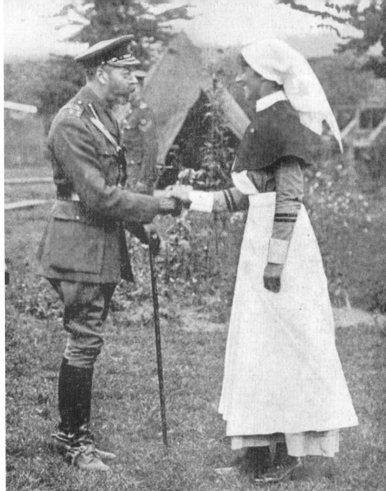

The King visits wounded officers.
40BP

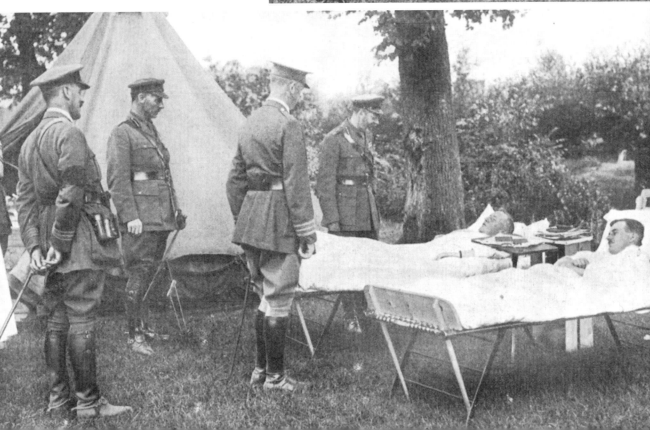

The King inspects a gun pit. 304GP

The King is given three cheers by Australian troops as he strides through their ranks. 63BP

Australians cheer the King. 56BP

On the battlefield Sir Henry Rawlinson points out a feature to the King and General Congreve, commander of XIII Corps. 56BP

The King and General Congreve. 307GP

The King examines the markings on the grave of an unknown British soldier. 155GP

The King in a captured German trench. 306GP

The King on the lip of a crater at Mametz. 82BP

The King joins some of his men at a church service. 39BP

His Royal Highness the Duke of Connaught reviewing the Guards in France, 1916.
362GPa & 361GPa
64BPa
64BP

HRH the Duke of Connaught calls for three cheers for the King. 359GP

HRH the Duke of Connaught inspects an Irish regiment. 65BP

General Sir Douglas Haig
introducing General Joffre to
Lieutenant-General Sir Pertab
Singh. 51BP 363GP

Prime Minister of New Zealand, Mr William Massey, investigates a German dugout. 348GP
British Prime Minister Herbert Asquith observing soldiers adjusting fuses on Stokes mortars. 299GP

Constant work repairing and widening roads on the Somme. 73BP

Wooden piles for bridge building. 352BP

Royal Fusiliers resting after the storming of La Boisselle. 131BP

Lancashire Fusiliers resting after the fighting. 24BP 23BP

Royal Warwickshires.   141BP 140BP

A battalion of The Loyal North Lancashire Regiment parading for the trenches. 143BP

Indian cavalry moving forward, 15 July, in readiness to exploit any breakthrough. 133BP 99BP

Indian cavalry waiting to advance.
98BP

Mametz Wood. 256GP

Mametz Wood. A Royal Field Artillery battery moves to a new position; an exchange of wit seems to be in progress – likely with reference to the camera. I GP/W022

German ammunition wagons destroyed by artillery fire near Mametz Wood.
66BP 67BP

A wrecked German
observation platform
in Mametz Wood.
257GP

German gun
abandoned in Mametz
Wood. The breech
mechanism has been
removed.
309GP

An abandoned German artillery piece. 310GP

German gun destroyed by a direct hit. 341GPXX

Wrecked German gun at Martinpuich. 334GP

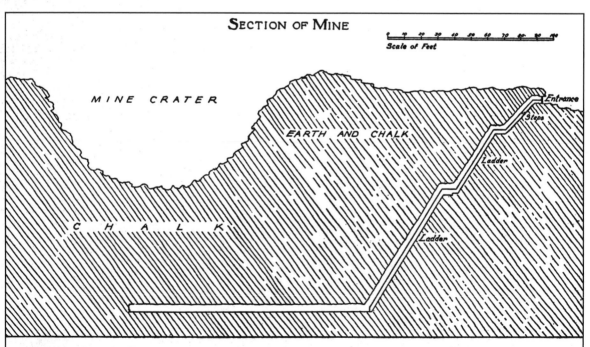

SECTION OF MINE

Scale of Feet

MINE CRATER

EARTH AND CHALK

CHALK

Entrance

Steps

Ladder

Ladder

This illustration shows a section of the mine which the Germans blew up under the base of the old crater at the moment of the advance in July.

A mine exploding under German trenches.   GBPMINE
British soldiers occupying a mine crater. Note the dugout. 235GP

Mine craters could be turned into strongpoints. British soldiers incorporating a crater into part of their defence line. 294GP

In some cases, during bad weather, many became deep ponds with slippery, unstable banks. 118BPa

The raised lip of a crater provided an excellent vantage point from which to observe the battlefield.
263GPA

Bottom of a La Boisselle mine crater. I GP/W023

Stretcher bearers
removing a
wounded man at
Thiepval.
321GP

Cookhouse
activity at
Thiepval.
27BP

View of the German-held village of Thiepval. 42BP

A novel form of battlefield signposting, two British Lee Enfield rifles. 42bpa

Australian machine
gun team passing a
work detail. 72BP

Sunken road
between La Boisselle
and Contalmaison.
I /GPW024

A Vickers Machine Gun company arrives by motorcycle and rushes into action during a training session on the Somme. Norton and BSA machines and combinations seem to be in evidence. 15BP

A loose fuel line rather than enemy action. 15BP

A Rolls-Royce armoured car. 286GP

A scene near Guillemont, a Rolls-Royce armoured car among the ambulances. Note the chains on the rear wheels to give traction through mud. 33BP

Trench-mortar bomb dump well behind the lines. 323GP

Trench-mortar bombs made ready for action and dispersed behind the firing position. 295GP

Trench-mortar being readied for firing from a specially constructed pit. 350GP

An artillery sergeant receiving a gift of a packet of cigarettes donated by a tobacco company. The gun is a 4.5-inch howitzer. 367 GP

Troops learning to work behind a smokescreen. 296 GP

Troops awaiting their turn to advance. Battle of Morval, 25 September. 344GP
Waiting to attack, 25 September 1916. 325GP

Main street in the village of Ginchy. 326GP

Advancing over the top and through a
captured communication trench. 259GP 260GP

Advancing 25 September. 37BP

Ready to begin the advance on the villages of Lesboeufs and Morval. 36BP

Prisoners being brought in. 105BP

Aid station at Guillemont. 146GP

Captured German trench smashed by bombardment. 10BP

Repairing and re-establishing a road over captured terrain. 314GP

German trench at Ginchy. 315GP

Main street of Guillemont. 317GP

The camera captures scenes of a twentieth century battlefield showing the results of shells and machine guns – torn ground and torn men.

l GP/W025
l GP-W028ok
l GP/W027

A German 77mm field gun position which has received a direct hit.
I GP/W029

Stretcher bearers bringing in a wounded comrade pass a dead horse with a severed neck.
1 GP/W030

German prisoners being used to carry wounded on stretchers away from the front line. Note one prisoner is carrying a rifle slung over his shoulder. 1 GP/W031

An extra large explosion causes heads to turn at this Main Dressing Station. I GP/W032

Main Dressing Station at Courcelette, September 1916. 34BP 132BP

German prisoners and the first appearance of the tank on the battlefield. | GP/W033
70BP

Smashed German trench at Morval. 74BP

Official photographers' convoy finds itself threatened by an enemy barage on Trones Wood, September 1916. IGP/W034

Trones Wood, September 1916. IGP/W035

Delville Wood 1916. A hand-written note on the back of this photograph reads:
A few scattered members of my own battalion, 16th King's Royal Rifle Corps, after the first few weeks of the battle on the Somme. This wood was thick with trees previous to the 1916 onslaught.
IGP/W036

Delville Wood. 320GP

Shelters in a wood. 53BP

A dud German shell and a warning sign. 71BP

Battalion cooks preparing hundreds of hot meals in appalling weather conditions.
79BP 346GP

The hot food dixies arrive at the front where a soldier samples the fare for the camera. I GP/W037

Officers at Bernafay Wood. I GP/W038

Soldiers of an Irish battalion being trucked to the rear following the taking of Guillemont. 25BP 298GP

Captured German machine guns being cleaned up for re-use. 342GPXX

Stretcher bearers moving up to the front. 342GPX

Bringing in wounded. I GP/W040

Bringing the wounded from Guillemont. I GP/W04I

Canadians wheel a wounded comrade to an Advance Dressing Station. 30GP
Walking wounded parade at a Casualty Clearing Station. 30GP

Indian cavalry despatch riders returning from the fighting around the village of Flers. A use found for the obsolescent charger. 43BP
A novel feature of the battlefield — the tank moving towards Flers. 345GP

Views of the village street of Flers. 21BP

Tank *D7* is stuck in a shell hole; three of the crew, wearing their distinctive helmets, can be seen taking shelter among the infantry. 1GP/W042

Bombs dropped from aircraft were another form of death making their debut. Crater caused by a missile dropped from a German aircraft. 281GP

Capture of Morval by men of the 5th Division, 25 September 1916. I GP/W043

112BPb

112BPd

112BPa

112BPc

Bringing in prisoners and wounded at Carnoy.   113BP

A wounded soldier being helped into an ambulance. 358GP
German wounded arriving at a prison camp. 302GP

An anti-aircraft gun in action at night. 153GP
A shell explosion at night with white-hot shrapnel causing a spectacular display. 52BP

Engineers moving up bridging supplies at dusk. 8BP
A view from the trenches on the night of 1 July 1916. 230GP

Spectacular display on the morning of the British attack of 15 September 1916. 106BP
A war horse and its rider against the early morning sky. 89BP

A De Havilland 'pusher' biplane taking off at Vert Galant airfield, British Fourth Army Aircraft Park.
238GP

Men of a West Indian regiment watching air activity. 241GP

No.3 Squadron flying Morane 'Parasols' from La Houssoye, September 1916. 312GP
No.32 Squadron pilots at Vert Galant, 1916. They are standing in front of a DH2, De Havilland Scout. 347GP

The shelled Basilica of Notre-Dame de Brebièresthe at Albert, three miles behind the front. The statue of Mary and the infant Jesus hanging from the tower gave rise to the superstition that whichever side in the conflict caused it to topple to the ground would lose the war. I GP/W044

Respiratory drill for these men of a Guards battalion. Poison gas attacks were yet another innovative feature of this first industrialised world war. 147GP

The village of Mensil, a short distance behind the British lines. I GP/W045
A Company Orderly Room carries on its duties in the open air. I GP/W046

This company of an infantry battalion catch up on sleep. Note the stacked rifles. I GP/W047

An artillery position with men taking a break. I GP/W048

Time out of the front line always meant being assigned work details. I GP/W050
Men of the King's Own Yorkshire Light Infantry, Mortar Section priming bombs. I GP/W049

A British Tommy finds comfort among the ruins of a French dwelling. 1GP/W051

A wiring party in the rain. 365GP

Men of a British Cyclist Company. Mounted troops often operated in a reconnaissance and communications role. I GP/W052

All hands to rescue a capsized ambulance. 320AGP

A battalion of the Middlesex Regiment on its way to the front. I GP/W084

Grass alight following
a large explosion.
396GP

Men resting in front
line 'funk' holes.
1 GP/W53

Reserves waiting to go up at Thiepval, September 1916.   I GP/W054

Walking wounded make their way to a Walking Wounded Collecting Station, September 1916.
I GP/W056

Tommies with prisoners. | GP/W055

Beaumont Hamel cratering through mining activity. I GP/W057
Very little left of the church at Beaumont Hamel. I GP/W058

The cemetery at Beaumont Hamel. Writing on the back of this photograph:
All that remained of the cemetery and village when the 51st Division on our right on November 13/16 took it. Square stone pile in the foreground is remainder of German monument to their 1914 fallen.
I GP/W059

The railway station
at Beaumont
Hamel.
GP/W055

The village of
Pozières after its
capture.
311GP

41BP

An officer's dugout with bedding and blankets out to dry. 322GP

Frost covered trees an early sign of winter. 397GP

Chapter Five

Somme Winter

With any further large scale offensive action on the Somme becoming impossible as the Franco-British armies bogged down in the increasingly severe weather, it became imperative that the sacrifice in human lives be justified. The British Empire had suffered 420,000 casualties and the French 204,000 against Germany's killed and injured of 465,000, making the Battle of the Somme the bloodiest engagement in history. How could this be explained away to the thousands of families who had lost their menfolk or had them maimed? Here is how it was done...

'ALTHOUGH THE HEAVY AUTUMN rains had prevented full advantage from being taken of the favourable situation created by our advance, at a time when we had good grounds for hoping that we were on the eve of securing yet more important successes, by the third week in November the three main objects with which we had commenced our offensive had already been achieved: Verdun had been relieved; the main German forces had been held on the Western Front; and the enemy's strength had been very considerably worn down.

"Any one of these three results," writes Sir Douglas Haig "is in itself sufficient to justify the Somme battle. The attainment of all three of them affords ample compensation for the splendid efforts of our troops and for the sacrifices made by ourselves and our Allies. They have brought us a long step forward towards the final victory of the Allied cause.

"The total number of prisoners taken by us in the Somme battle between the 1st of July and the 18th of November is just over 38,000 including over 800 officers. During the same period we captured 29 heavy guns, 96 field-guns and field howitzers, 136 trench-mortars and 514 machine guns.

"So far as these results are due to the action of the British forces, they have been obtained by troops the vast majority of whom had been raised and trained during the war. Many of them, especially amongst the drafts sent to replace wastage, counted their service by months, and gained in the Somme battle their first experience of war. We were compelled either to use hastily-trained and inexperienced officers and men, or else to defer the offensive until we had trained them. In the latter case, we should have failed our Allies. That these troops should have accomplished so much under such conditions, and against an army and a nation whose chief concern for so many years had been preparation for war, constitutes a feat to which the history of our nation records no equal. The difficulties and hardships cheerfully overcome, and the endurance, determination and invincible courage shown in meeting them, can hardly be imagined by those who have not had personal experience of the battle, even though they have themselves seen something of war."'

Delivering waders as the Great Push begins to bog down. I GP/W061

Moving supplies in deteriorating conditions.
20BP 342GP

Hitching a lift away
from the trenches.
380GP

Bowls of hot soup
for these Royal
Artillery riders.
369GP

Top: Ammunition limber and crew await means of haulage. 384GP

Above: The mules arrive. 381GP

Left: On the move. 379GP

A mule receives a clean up after having been rescued from the mud. 386GP
Canadians watering their mounts. 393GP

With the roads to artillery positions impassable mules loaded with up to ten rounds each are used to transport shells. 45BP

Royal Engineers bringing up a pontoon for bridging a river. 32BP

Repositioning an 8-inch howitzer through worsening conditions on the ground.
46BP

When 8-inch howitzers required moving the American-built Holt agricultural tractor with petrol engine and crawler tracks did the job. 44BP

A petrol-driven tractor reverses to hook up an 8-inch howitzer. 382GP

A six-cylinder Daimler engine tractor hauling ammunition. 375GP

Early Christmas messages of 'goodwill' for the Germans (not that they would be able to read them) chalked on shells for the camera man to record:

Above: 'Xmas Greetings from Canada' goes on an 8-inch shell.

Left: 'A Busting Time this Christmas 1916' chalked on a 5-inch shell.

Once a British communications trench, now a small stream. 389GP
Fighting another losing battle – bailing out on the Somme. 385GP

Beaumont Hamel November 1916. The back of the photograph below reads:
A portion of the old German front line at Beaumont Hamel in 1916. Notice heavy barbed wire entanglements and muddy state of the ground.   I GP/W066 I GP/W067

Barbed wire entanglements erected by the Germans at Beaumont Hamel, November 1916. I GP/W068

A bloodsoaked German prisoner is being helped by a British army chaplain. 383GP

British soldiers returning from leave; one is carrying a concertina and appears to have been playing it as they marched along. 373GP

A wrecked watermill at St Pierre Divion. 377GP

British and French soldiers sorting through captured German rifles. 387GP

Captured German helmets worn for the camera. 343GP

With the help of his damaged steel helmet a wounded Tommy shows how he received his head wound. 353GP

Men of a pioneer battalion repairing a road. 371GP

Entente Cordiale – a French and British soldier exchange greetings. 356GP

An officer's winter quarters. 13BP

Frozen and windswept Somme landscape in November 1916. 12BP 77BP

Taking water from the River Ancre in the winter of 1916. 7BP
Manhandling a cart of heavy shells. 14BP

Washing the mud off rifles in the flooded Ancre valley. 77BPa

A Company on the march with the cookers keeping the food hot ready for the order to halt. 19BP

Pioneers digging drainage ditches alongside a supply road. 68BP

Drinking water collecting point. 108BP

NOTICE
DIXIES & TINS TO
BE FILLED AT THIS
TANK.

Soldiers in winter-wear goat skin coats. 293GP

Signallers ensuring communication on the Ancre. 399GP

These men of a pioneer battalion handing in their equipment after a work period. I GP/W063

Ancre Valley, November 1916; unloading ammunition. | GP/W064

Royal Artillery moving 60-pounder guns by horse teams. I GP/W065

The mill at Beaucourt-sur-Ancre. 391GP

French and British soldiers clearing up a German trench at St Pierre Divion. 374GP

British troops on the Ancre. 1 GP/W069 48BP

Men of the 17th London Regiment walking along the Ancre Valley, October 1916. I GP/W070

Highlanders with a captured German mortar near St Pierre Divion, November 1916. I GP/W071

Working party at Bernafay Wood, November 1916. 1 GP/W075
Abandoned German equipment at St Pierre Divion, November 1916. 78BP

I GP/W062
28BP

In November 1916 the Great Push ended in the grip of winter. IBP

Somme Chronology

December 1915: France, Britain, Russia and Italy agree to simultaneous attacks on three fronts in the summer of 1916. Sir Douglas Haig, appointed C-in-C, BEF.

General Joffre, C-in-C French Army, proposes joint offensive on a sixty-mile front astride the River Somme.

February 1916: Joffre and Haig agree on a plan for a joint summer offensive starting on or about 1 July. The French advise Haig about an impending German attack on Verdun.

Haig orders General Rawlinson to take over planning of attack on the Somme.

German Fifth Army attacks the French XXX Corps at Verdun.

March 1916: General Rawlinson appointed to command the British Fourth Army.

Haig decides to copy German method of artillery bombardment employed at Verdun to clear the ground for an infantry advance in the coming attack on the Somme.

British Fourth Army relieves French Tenth Army.

Joffre, Sir Douglas Haig and Foch 1916. I GP/W080
General Sir Henry Rawlinson and General Sir Douglas Haig at Fourth Army HQ, Querrieu, July 1916. I GP/W080

April 1916: Rawlinson submits his plan to Haig suggesting an advance of between 1,000 and 3,000 yards on a 20,000 yard front running from Serre to Maricourt. His declared intention, to 'kill as many Germans as possible with the least loss to ourselves'.

Rawlinson is asked to consider 'probable opportunities' for the use of cavalry in the offensive. Joffre informs Haig that the number of French divisions available for the joint offensive has fallen from thirty-nine to thirty.

May 1916: Haig and Rawlinson agree on objectives and length of bombardment is set at four days.

Joffre tells Haig French divisions available have fallen from thirty to twenty-six. Rawlinson warned he may have to attack without French support.

Joffre informs Haig only twenty French divisions now available for the joint offensive.

June 1916: Joffre confirms Saturday 1 July as the preferred start date for the British-French offensive.

6th - Joffre writes to Haig talking about the need for a battle of attrition – a battle of *duree prolongee*. Also states that the number of French divisions to be involved now reduced from twenty to twelve.

Joffre asks for Somme date to be brought forward to 25 June to relieve pressure on Verdun with the bombardment to start on Tuesday, 20 June.

Haig informs all Army commanders that he believes the capture of the German second line positions is almost certain and that, if this happens,

> 'Our advance will be pressed forward eastwards far enough to enable our cavalry to push through into open country. Our objective will then be to turn northwards, taking the enemy's lines in flank and reverse. Should an advance beyond this position not be possible then then most profitable course will probably be to transfer our main efforts rapidly to another portion of the British front.'

Joffre asks for the attack to be postponed until either 29 June or 1 July. Haig agrees to 29 June.

20th - GHQ raises concerns with Rawlinson over ammunition expenditure for bombardment.

21st - Rawlinson agrees to reduce the intensity so as to save shells for later fighting.

24th - U Day, first day of British/French bombardment.

25th - V Day, bombardment.

26th - W Day, bombardment.

27th - X Day, bombardment.

28th - Y Day, fifth day of bombardment.

29th - Z Day, planned date for attack. (Postponed because of bad weather.)

30th - Y1 Day. (British/French bombardment extended).

July 1916 1st - Z Day. Battle of the Somme STARTS at 7.30am.

Combined Franco-British attack on a twenty-five mile front north and south of the River Somme. British capture the villages of Montauban and Mametz. The French attack towards Peronne and reach outskirts of the villages of Hardecourt and Curlu. North-west of the Albert-Bapaume road the British make little progress against the German defences except for a small gain at the Leipzig Redoubt to the south of Thiepval. They fail to capture the villages of Gommecourt, Serre, Beaumont Hamel, Thiepval and la Boisselle. On the first day 57,470 British and Newfoundland soldiers are killed or wounded.

2nd: Village of Fricourt is re-captured by the Germans. Rawlinson's estimate of casualties is 30,000.

3rd: Village of La Boisselle is captured and part of the village of Ovillers.

4th: Bernafay Wood cleared.

7th: Village of Contalmaison captured as well as German strongpoint Leipzig Redoubt.

8th: British gain a hold in Trones Wood.

10th: Fierce fighting in Trones Wood. Progress in the fight for Mametz Wood.

11th: Contalmaison holds against German counter-attacks. Continued fighting in Trones and Mametz Woods.

12th: Mametz Wood finally captured.

14th: British attack and capture the villages of Longueval and Bazentin le Petit and take the whole of Trones Wood.

15th: Battle for Delville Wood begins. Attempts to capture High Wood fail.

16th: British withdraw from High Wood.

17th: East of Longueval German position at Waterlot Farm taken. Village of Ovillers completely cleared of Germans. Battle of Bazentin Ridge ends.

18th: Germans make strong counter-attacks at Longueval and Delville Wood.

19th: German counter-attacks on Waterlot Farm and Trones Wood repulsed.

20th: Longueval and Delville Wood fighting continues.

21st: Fighting at High Wood. Haig visits Rawlinson and impresses on him the need to capture the village of Guillemont.

22nd: Heavy fighting on the front Pozieres to Guillemont.

23rd: Second phase of the Somme battle with fighting in and around the village of Pozieres. British recapture the whole of Longueval but the Germans counter-attack to retake the northern part of the village. The outskirts of Guillemont change hands twice. Rawlinson notes in his diary that the Germans had not relinquished their attacks in Verdun although they had thinned their line so as to release troops for the Somme battle.

24th: Fighting at Pozieres continues and the Germans counter-attack at High Wood and Guillemont.

25th: Series of British attacks against High Wood end. The Germans counter-attack in the Longueval and Bazentin areas. Pozieres is almost entirely in Allied hands and the British push along the Albert-Bapaume road.

26th: Entire village of Pozieres in Allied hands.

27th: British attack and gain in Delville Wood. Fighting continues near Pozieres and at Longueval.

28th: British capture Longueval and Delville Wood and make further progress near Pozieres.

29th: German attempts to retake Delville Wood fail.

30th: British make progress east of Waterlot Farm and Trones Wood.

31st: Fighting for Guillemont continues. RFC bomb Martinpuich.

August 1st: North of Bazentin le Petit the German counter-attack is repulsed. Heavy fighting continues at Verdun.

2nd: German attack on Delville Wood repulsed. More heavy fighting at Verdun.

3rd: The British gain ground west of Pozieres and the French progress at Verdun.

4th: Allies gain the German Second Line system on a front of 2,000 yards to the north of Pozieres. German counter-attacks at Verdun repulsed.

5th: British advance their line near Pozieres.

7th: British attack outskirts of Guillemont. German attacks to the north and north-east of Pozieres repulsed. The French progress at Verdun.

8th: British fighting at Guillemont continues. The station is captured and the northern parts of the village.

9th: Renewed British attacks against Guillemont fail.

10th: King George V visits the front and Rawlinson takes him to the craters at Bois Francais. The King informs Rawlinson of a move to remove Haig by among others Lord French, Winston Churchill and F. E. Smith. The British make progress to the

King George V arrives at Fourth Army headquarters 10 August 1916. ! GP/W082

north-west of Pozieres.

12th: British advance on a mile front north-west of Pozieres.

15th: The King returns to England after his visit to the Western Front.

16th: British advance west and south-west of Guillemont.

18th: Ground gained by the British towards the villages of Ginchy and Guillemont.

19th: British gain ground in Thiepval Ridge area.

20th: Germans counter-attack at Thiepval.

22nd: Two determined counter-attacks by the Germans south of Thiepval are beaten off.

23rd: Fighting continues south of Thiepval. Strong German attacks at Guillemont repulsed. Rawlinson learns that twelve tanks have arrived.

24th: Further progress by the British towards Thiepval and part of Delville Wood. German attacks to the west of Ginchy driven off.

25th: German attack south of Thiepval repulsed, the enemy driven out of Delville Wood and a line established along the north-east edge.

26th: Germans counter-attack near Thiepval. Rawlinson sees the tanks in training and is impressed.

28th: Haig's Chief of Staff, General Kiggell, visits Rawlinson to discuss how best to use the new weapon – tanks – in battle. Rawlinson favours caution in their use.

31st: Fierce German attacks between Ginchy and High Wood repulsed.

September 1st: German attacks at High Wood fail but they are back again in the eastern side of Delville Wood.

2nd: Rawlinson inspects the tanks again and is not pleased with their training and handling.

3rd: The Battle for Delville Wood ends and also that of Pozieres Ridge. The Battle for Guillemont is at last won by the British, but Ginchy is first taken and then lost. Continuous fighting towards Falfemont Farm and High Wood.

4th: Another British attack on Falfemont Farm fails.

5th: East of Guillemont the Allied line is carried forward 1,500 yards and most of Leuze Wood is captured. The Allies now occupy the whole of the German second line. During the night Falfemont Farm is taken.

6th: Village of Guillemont consolidated and the British advance to Ginchy completed. Leuze Wood is secured.

9th: Ginchy falls to the British. Trenches also taken to the north and east of Leuze Wood.

10th: The Germans counter-attack at Ginchy but are repulsed. The British line to the east of Guillemont is advanced. Rawlinson attends a conference which features the role of the tanks in the forthcoming battle.

12th: French take the area to the south of Combles as far as the River Somme.

Intense British preparatory bombardment.

13th: The French progress to the south-east of Combles.

14th: British storm trenches to the south-east of Thiepval and take the *Wonderwork*. Haig urges Rawlinson to attack the village of Martinpuich and that the cavalry should be pushed out towards le Sars.

15th: Third phase of the Battle of the Somme begins and an advance on a six mile front to a depth of 2,000 to 3,000 yards is achieved. Flers, Martinpuich, Courcelette and High Wood are captured; tanks made their debut in battle. The French Army makes progress to the south of Rancourt and captures a system of trenches north of the Priez Farm. Rawlinson pleased with the part played by the tanks in the advance.

16th: Germans counter-attack at Courcelette but the British gain some territory. Danube Trench and Mouquet Farm are taken.

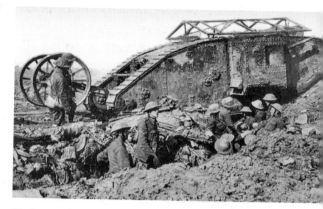

Tanks used in warfare for the first time. 15 September 1916.

18th: Continuous rain all day. The Sixth Division take the troublesome Quadrilateral between Ginchy and Bouleux Wood to a depth of a thousand yards.

21st: New Zealanders capture Cough Drop Alley and a good bit of the Flers Line, whilst the 1st Division capture Starfish Trench.

22nd: Battle of Flers-Courcelette ends.

25th: Successful day for the British, both Lesboeufs and Morval are captured. The village of Combles is hemmed in by the Allies. The Battle of Morval begins.

26th: Combles falls to the Allies and Thiepval is finally captured. The Battle for Thiepval Ridge begins. The British storm Guedecourt.

27th: British attack Stuff Redoubt and advance to the north of Flers, east of Eaucourt L'Abbaye.

28th: British attack the *Schwaben* Redoubt on the crest of the Thiepval Plateau, and capture most of it. They advance to the north and north-east of Courcelette, between Martinpuich and Guedecourt. The French make progress at Morval and the Battle of Morval Ridge ends.

29th: British capture German stronghold at Destremont Farm.

30th: Thiepval Ridge is captured except for part of *Schwaben* Redoubt.

October 1st: The Battle of Transloy Ridge and Ancre Heights begins. British attack on the line Eaucourt-le Sars (on the Albert-Bapaume Road) and capture their objectives on a front of 3,000 yards. Eaucourt is occupied.

2nd: Germans counter-attack in Eaucourt and the British fail to hold le Sars.

3rd: British recover Eaucourt L'Abbaye.

5th: British advance north-west of Eaucourt and the French make progress east of Morval.

6th: Haig expresses the view that he wants the battle to go on until the winter unless the weather makes it impossible.

7th: The British and French advance on the Albert-Bapaume Road. The British advance a thousand yards and capture le Sars. The French advance to the north-east of Morval and reach to within 200 yards of Sailly.

8th: British line is advanced north and east of Courcelette. Germans attack and regain some trenches. The French have success at Sailly-Saillisel. The Canadians capture and then lose Regina Trench and the Quadrilateral strong point.

9th: British make progress to towards the Butte de Warlencourt.

11th: Battle of the Ancre Heights ends and the French repulse German attacks at the Bois de Chaulnes.

12th: British attack on a four mile front between Eaucourt and Bapaume.

14th: Rawlinson in his diary considers that the weather will bring the battle to a close soon. Since the casualties on 1 July a further 40,000 casualties are estimated by Rawlinson.

15th: British make progress in the neighbourhood of the *Schwaben* Redoubt and Thiepval.

17th: Haig confers with Rawlinson about future battle plans.

18th: Battle of the Transloy Ridges ends.

19th: German attacks against the *Schwaben* and Stuff Redoubts on the Thiepval Plateau repulsed.

21st: British advance on a line between the *Schwaben* Redoubt and le Sars and take many prisoners.

23rd: British advance towards le Transloy and capture a thousand yards of enemy trenches.

24th: French have success at Verdun when they retake Fort Douaumont and capture 3,500 prisoners.

27th: Ground conditions are so bad that Rawlinson considers that it would be a physical impossibility for the infantry to advance.

30th: Heavy rain makes the condition of the roads worse than ever. The French take trenches north-west of Sailly-Saillisel.

31st: Road and trench conditions are very bad and the area around Guedecourt is waterlogged. Rawlinson despairs of a further advance.

November 1st: German counter-attack against Sailly-Saillisel is repulsed. Allies advance north-east of Lesboeufs. Germans evacuate Fort Vaux at Verdun.

2nd: British capture trenches east of Guedecourt.

5th: French in possession of Fort Vaux (Verdun). The British make some progress at the Butte de Warlencourt and towards le Transloy. The Anzac Corps gain and then lose Bayonet Trench.

6th: French progress near St Pierre Vaast Wood.

7th: British progress to the east of the Butte de Warlencourt.

8th: Germans repulsed at Saillisel.

10th: British capture the east portion of Regina Trench to the north of Thiepval. The French capture several German trenches to the north-east of Lesboeufs. Rawlinson visits Ginchy and Delville Wood. He sees for himself how appalling the roads are beyond Ginchy.

13th: Battle of the Ancre begins and Beaumont Hamel is stormed by the British. They capture St Pierre Divion, and Beaumont Hamel, and over 3,000 prisoners. The beginning of the fourth phase of the Battle of the Somme.

14th: British capture Beaucourt and advance to the east of the Butte de Warlencourt. The number of prisoners taken in the two days reaches 5,200.

15th: German counter-attacks fail.

16th: British extend their line eastwards from Beaucourt and retreat from part of the ground to the east of the Butte de Warlencourt.

17th: Further advances on the Ancre.

18th: British advance north and south of the Ancre and reach the outskirts of Grandcourt. The operations end and the Battle of the Somme is over.

In March 1917, the Germans carried out a strategic withdrawal to straighten out their line. This new defensive position became known as the Hindenburg Line. British troops advance to occupy the vacated ground near the once German strongpoint at the village of Serre. 1 GP/W083